ELEMENTARY PIANO LEVEL 1B

LEVEL 1B

WunderKeys Elementary Piano Level 1B by Andrea and Trevor Dow
Copyright © 2019 Teach Music Today Learning Solutions
www.teachpianotoday.com and www.wunderkeys.com

WELCOME

"I hated piano lessons as a child." Every time an adult says those words, our hearts break a little. So our mission with WunderKeys is simple: to make kids fall in love with piano lessons. No one should grow up to utter those seven awful words.

To help kids become piano-loving adults, a method book must: 1. be developmentally appropriate and perfectly paced, 2. have activities that allow students to engage with notated music in unique and creative ways, and 3. contain story-based excitement that makes kids connect with music. WunderKeys succeeds at all three!

Elementary Piano Level 1B is the final book in our level 1 series and is an immersive musical experience divided into eight units. In what can only be described as magic, we've packed Level 1B with sight reading, technical exercises, piano games, and rockin' rhythm duets while still providing as much repertoire as a traditional method book.

Thirty years from now, your former students will be able to say the seven words we long to hear: "I loved piano lessons as a child."

Andrea and Trevor Dow

The Nitty Gritty

WunderKeys Elementary Piano Level 1B is the final book in our level 1 series. In this book your students will...

1. Gain an understanding of accidentals by identifying and playing notes affected by sharps and flats.

2. Reinforce note reading in C five-finger scales and G five-finger scales.

3. Explore major chords and minor chords in blocked and broken forms.

4. Improve bilateral abilities and explore mid-piece hand movements.

5. Continue an exploration of rhythm with an introduction to eighth notes.

1. With your right hand (RH) 1 on Middle C, use your RH 4 to play F. Now use your RH 4 to play the black key directly above F. This key is called F sharp. It is a **half-step higher** than F.

2. With your LH 1 on Middle C, use your LH 4 to play G. Now use your LH 4 to play the black key directly above G. The key you just played is called G sharp. It is a half-step higher than G.

3. The distance from one key to the very next black or white key is called a half step. On each image, name the marked key and then name (and point to) the key that is a half-step higher.

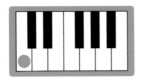

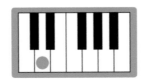

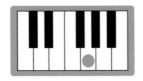

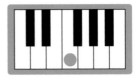

On the piano, place your RH 1 on Middle C. Practice playing F and then F sharp. Continue alternating between these two keys. Next, place your LH 5 on Bass C. Practice alternating between F and F sharp. Finally, place your LH 1 on Middle C. Practice alternating between G and G sharp.

In music, a sharp sign in front of a note tells you to play the key that is a half-step higher.

A sharp sign looks like this:

The two excerpts in Row 1 are **almost identical**. With your RH 1 on Middle C, play the first excerpt. Now look at the second excerpt. The sharp sign is telling you to play the key that is a half-step higher than F (F sharp) instead of playing F. Play this excerpt using your RH 4 to reach to F sharp. Practice playing with sharps in Rows 2 to 5.

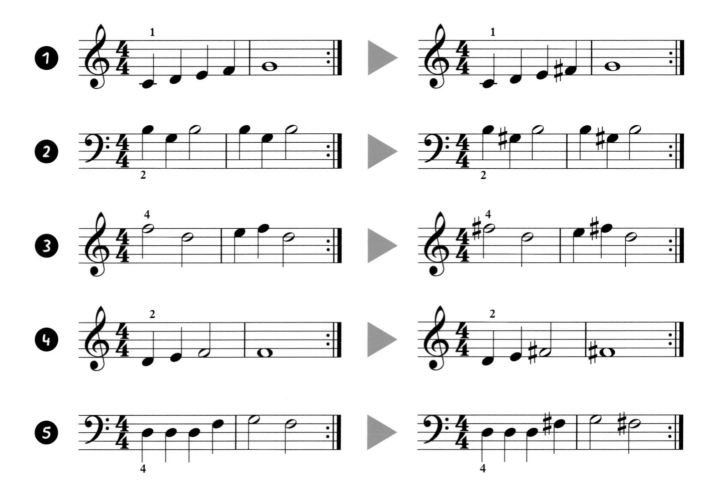

Can you point to the measures below with notes **affected** by sharp signs? Practice these measures before you begin this activity. Beginning at the giant and ending at the foxes, play the four measures of music that rest on the dotted path. Next, I will use a colored crayon to draw a new four-measure path that begins at the giant and ends at the foxes. Try playing along the new path. **Let's play again.**

NOTE-READING ALERT!

A sharp sign can be placed on individual notes and on notes that make up harmonic intervals.

In Exercise 2, point to a **harmonic interval** with a sharp sign. Name the bottom and top notes. Next, play the harmonic interval as it would be played if it didn't have a sharp sign. Now play the harmonic interval as written.

technical EXERCISES

MUSIC-MARKING ALERT! Look at Exercise 3. Can you find a new music marking? *Rit.* stands for *ritardando* and tells you to gradually slow down until the end of a piece. Practice playing *ritardando* in Exercise 3.

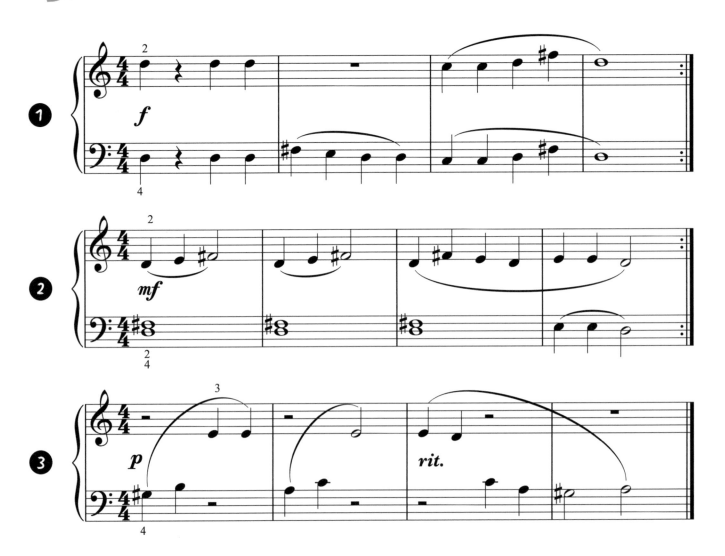

ear-training EXERCISE

Game Instructions: Watch and listen as I play a half step. Watch and listen as I play a whole step. Next, let's start our game.

Sit on the floor with this book, a red crayon, and a blue crayon. Place a finger over any circle and then listen as I play a half step or a whole step. Lift your finger off the circle. If the letter label on the circle **matches** the step I played (H = half step, W = whole step), color the circle red. If the letter label does not match the step I played, color the circle blue. Let's keep playing until there are three circles colored red (you win) or three circles colored blue (I win).

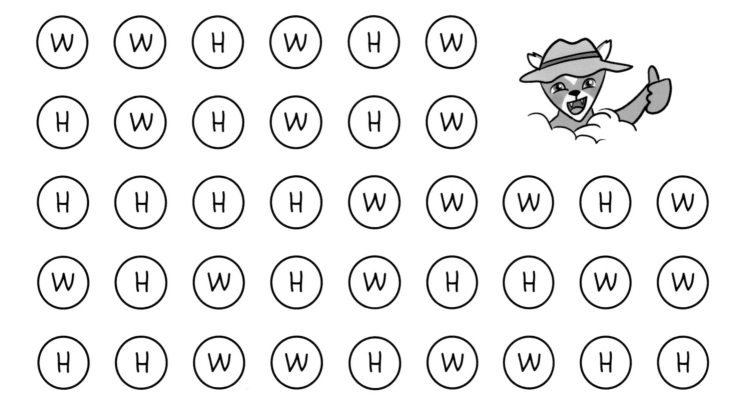

Let's play a Rhythm Duet! To begin, practice the body percussion below. Stem-down notes are performed by tapping both hands on your lap. Stem-up notes are performed by clapping your hands together. Next, I will play the music as an accompaniment while you perform the body percussion **four times**. Let's switch roles.

FEE FI FALLING

Floating

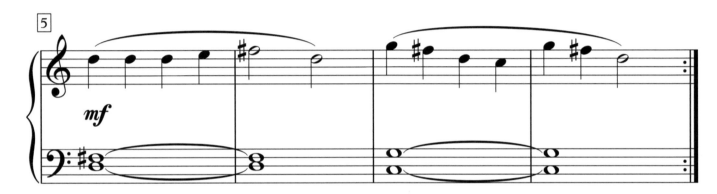

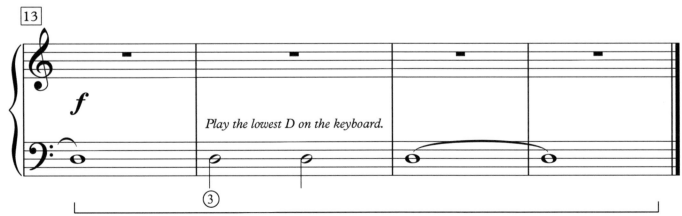

Play the lowest D on the keyboard.

THE GOLDEN HARP

*ALERT! Check your
starting position.*

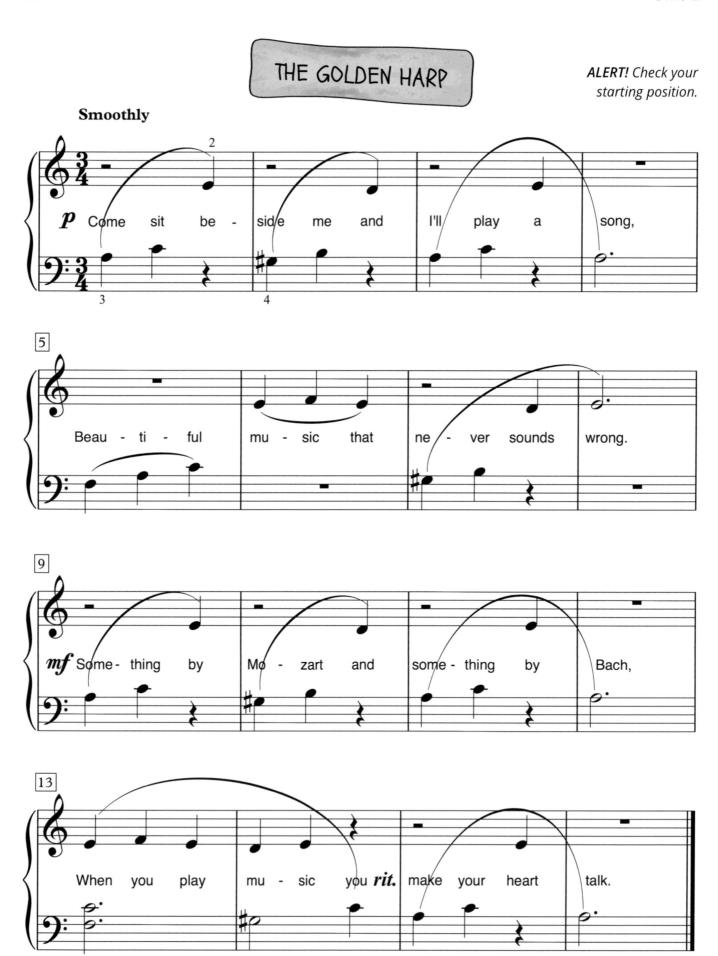

let's get STARTED

1. With your RH 1 on Middle C, use your RH 3 to play E. Now use your RH 3 to play the key that is a **half-step lower** than E. The key you just played is called E flat.

2. With your LH 1 on Middle C, use your LH 2 to play B. Now use your LH 2 to play the key that is a half-step lower than B. The key you just played is called B flat.

3. On each image, name the **marked key** and then name (and point to) the key that is a half-step lower.

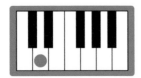

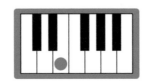

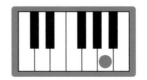

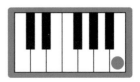

On the piano, place your RH 1 on Middle C. Practice playing E and then E flat. Continue alternating between these two keys. Next, place your LH 5 on Bass C. Practice alternating between E and E flat. Finally, place your LH 1 on Middle C. Practice alternating between B and B flat.

In music, a flat sign in front of a note tells you to play the key that is a half-step lower.

A flat sign looks like this:

The two excerpts in Row 1 are **almost identical**. With your RH 1 on Middle C, play the first excerpt. Now look at the second excerpt. The flat sign is telling you to play the key that is a half-step lower than E (E flat) instead of playing E. Play this excerpt using your RH 3 to reach to E flat. Practice playing with flats in Rows 2 to 5.

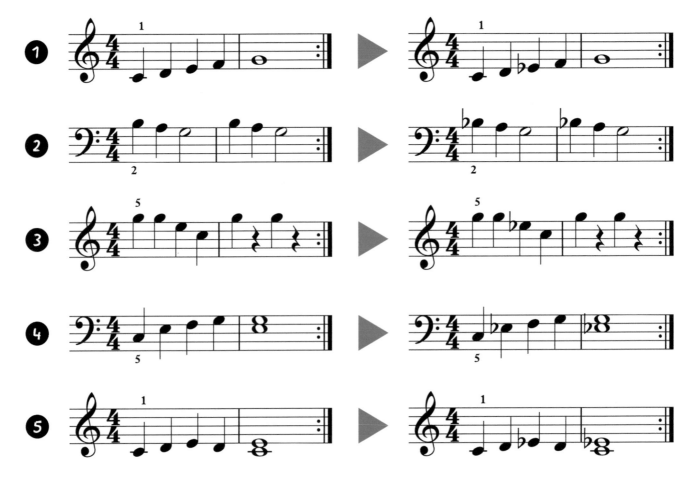

Can you point to the measures below with notes affected by flat signs? Practice these measures before you begin this activity. Beginning at the van and ending at the grasshopper, play the four measures of music that rest on the dotted path. Next, I will use a crayon to draw a new four-measure path that begins at the van and ends at the grasshopper. Try playing along the new path. **Let's play again.**

Before you play, read this!

Look at Exercise 1. Point to every note affected by a flat sign. Next, I will point to a measure in Exercise 1. Play the measure without the flat sign and then play the measure with the flat sign. Next, I will point to a new measure so you can play again.

Let's repeat this activity with Exercises 2 and 3.

technical EXERCISES

MUSIC-MARKING ALERT! Look at Exercise 3. Can you find the new music marking? A *fermata* above a note tells you to hold that note for longer than its rhythmic value. Practice playing the *fermata* in Exercise 3.

ear-training EXERCISE

Let's practice listening for **sharps and flats**. To begin, I will secretly choose five numbers between 1 and 36, record them on a slip of paper, and hide the paper until the game is over.

Next, close your eyes as I name and play a white key *(Teacher Note: choose only D, G, or A)* and then play a key that is a half-step higher or a half-step lower. Tell me the name of the second key I played and then roll a die. If the second key was a sharp, color a number of **squares** below that corresponds to the value on the die. If the second key was a flat, color a number of **circles** below that corresponds to the value on the die. Let's play three more rounds.

After all rounds are complete, I will reveal the secret numbers. Examine the numbers inside each shape below. Score yourself one point for every colored shape that contains a secret number.

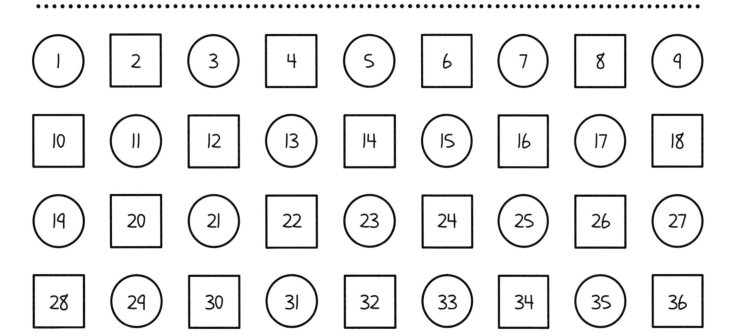

Let's play a Rhythm Duet! To begin, practice the body percussion below. Stem-down notes are performed by tapping both hands on your lap. Stem-up notes are performed by clapping your hands together. Next, I will play the music as an accompaniment while you perform the body percussion **four times**. Let's switch roles.

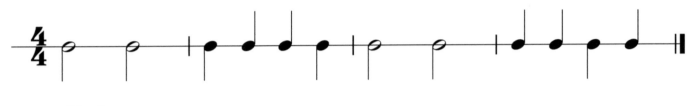

Lively

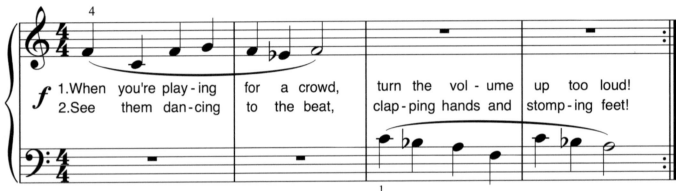

1.When you're play-ing for a crowd, turn the vol-ume up too loud!
2.See them dan-cing to the beat, clap-ping hands and stomp-ing feet!

Crank up your mu - sic! *mp* Watch them danc-ing in a line.

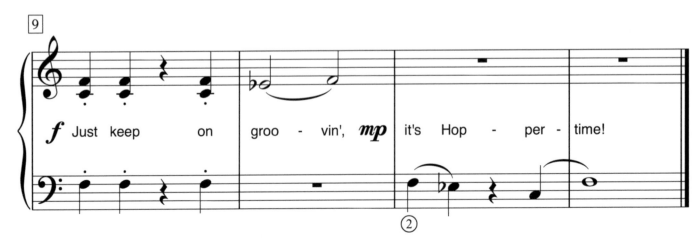

Just keep on groo - vin', *mp* it's Hop - per - time!

WINTER'S WORK

Flowing

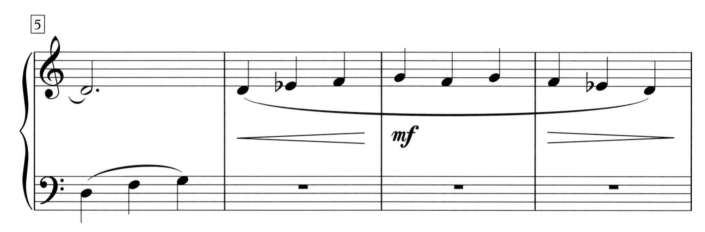

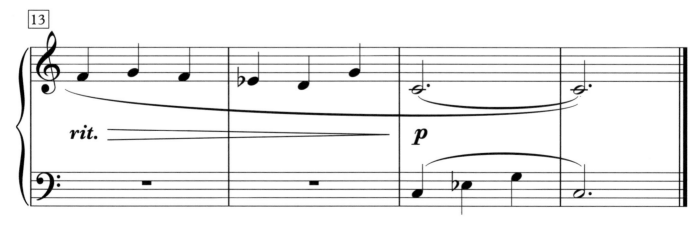

HOPPERTIME

let's get STARTED

1 Sharp signs and flat signs are special music symbols called accidentals. Let's learn about a **special rule** involving accidentals. When an accidental appears in a measure of music, it affects the note it is attached to as well as any more occurrences of the same note in the same measure. It cannot, however, have an effect on notes in the next measure.

2 Look at the first measure below. Name the note with the sharp sign. Using a colored pencil, circle notes in the same measure that are affected by the sharp sign. Next, play the measure. Repeat this activity with the remaining measures.

Look at the music below. I will point to a note with a flat sign. Can you name the note and then play its corresponding key on the piano?

Next, point to a measure of music below that has three notes affected by a flat sign. Point to a measure of music below that has two notes affected by a flat sign.

Finally, practice the **sight-reading activity** below.

Beginning at the fox and ending at the gingerbread man, play the four measures of music that rest on the dotted path. Next, I will use a colored crayon to draw a new four-measure path that begins at the fox and ends at the gingerbread man. Try playing along the new path. **Let's play again.**

HATTIE PLAYS BACH. THE GINGERBREAD MAN BAKES A MOTORBIKE.

HATTIE PLAYS STRAVINSKY. THE GINGERBREAD MAN COOKS A SKULLCAP.

HATTIE PLAYS GERSHWIN. THE GINGERBREAD MAN GRABS SOME GAS.

technical EXERCISES

NEW SKILL ALERT! The third exercise has accented notes in the second measure. An accent marking means that you play the corresponding notes louder than the other notes in the exercise.

THE GINGERBREAD MAN IS READY TO CRUISE.

THIS COOKIE'S NO ROOKIE.

Sit on the floor with this book. Place a coin over the gingerbread man. Listen as I play *legato* sounds, *staccato* sounds, or *accented* sounds. Move your coin one space to the left if only *staccato* was played, one space to the right if only *legato* was played, and one space forward if only *accents* were played.

I will keep playing musical excerpts until your coin lands on the **red circle** (you win) or a **fox** (you lose). If your coin lands on a green circle, it is returned to the gingerbread man and play continues.

ear-training **EXERCISE**

Note to Teachers: This game requires you to improvise musical excerpts containing only *legato* sounds, only *staccato* sounds, or only *accented* sounds.

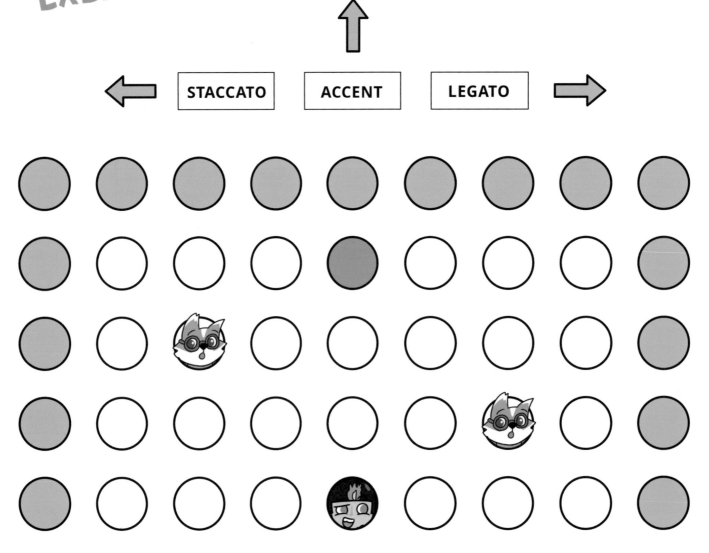

Let's play a Rhythm Duet! To begin, practice Body Percussions 1 and 2 below. Stem-down notes are performed by tapping both hands on your lap. Stem-up notes are performed by clapping your hands together. Next, I will play the music as an accompaniment while you perform Body Percussion 1 (don't forget the repeat sign). Let's try again with Body Percussion 2. Finally, let's switch roles.

CAN'T CATCH ME

Sneaking

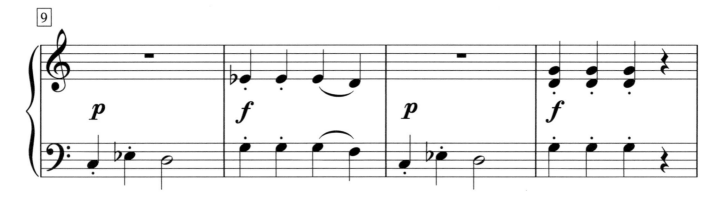

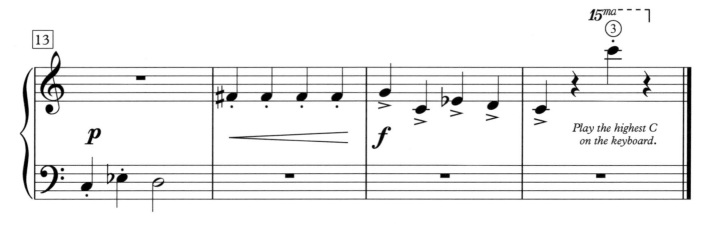

Play the highest C on the keyboard.

TIME'S UP

ALERT! Check your
starting position.

Grieg, arr. by Andrea Dow

Note: When using the teacher duet, the student part is played one octave higher.

FREE WHEELIN'

Groovin'

Beethoven, arr. by Andrea Dow

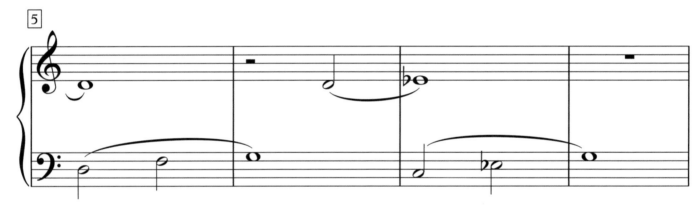

① In this lesson we're going to learn about **chords**. But before we can do that we have to learn about C five-finger scales. There are C major five-finger scales and C minor five-finger scales. They can be written on the bass staff or the treble staff.

② Practice the C major five-finger scales on the staves below. Next, look at the letters below each note. These are called **Roman Numerals.** These letters represent numbers (I = 1, II = 2, III = 3, IV = 4, V = 5). Each note in a five-finger scale is numbered with a Roman Numeral. I will call out a note name in the C major five-finger scale. Can you use its Roman Numeral to tell me its number name?

I (1)   II (2)   III (3)   IV (4)   V (5)

I (1)   II (2)   III (3)   IV (4)   V (5)

With your LH 5 on Bass C, play the I and V notes of the C major five-finger scale at the same time. As you know, this is called a harmonic interval of a fifth.

Next, with your LH 5 on Bass C, play the I, III and V notes of the C major five-finger scale at the same time. This is called a **C major chord.** A chord is similar to a harmonic interval but occurs when three notes are stacked and played at the same time.

Can you point to all of the C major chords below?

Beginning at Granny and ending at the wolf, play the four measures of music that rest on the dotted path. Next, I will use a colored crayon to draw a new four-measure path that begins at Granny and ends at the wolf. Try playing along the new path. **Let's play again.**

pick-a-path
SIGHT READING

technical EXERCISES

THEORY TIME! If a flat sign is placed on the III note of the C major five-finger scale, it becomes a C minor five-finger scale. If a flat sign is placed on the III note of a C major chord, it becomes a C minor chord. Practice playing these minor sounds in Exercise 3.

Listen as I play a C major chord or a C minor chord. Locate the box below that corresponds to the chord I played, and roll a die. Inside the selected box, **color a numbered circle** that corresponds to the number rolled. If all circles that correspond to the number rolled have already been colored in previous rounds, draw an **X** over one red circle.

Next, repeat the procedure above until all of the circles inside one of the two boxes are colored or until there is an **X** over every red circle.

ear-training EXERCISE

Winning the Game: The student wins the game if all of the circles in one of the two boxes are colored before an **X** is drawn over every red circle.

MAJOR

MINOR

MAJOR			MINOR		
1	5	3	2	1	3
3	M	1	5	m	2
2	4	4	1	4	6

Let's play a Rhythm Duet! To begin, practice Body Percussions 1 and 2 below. Stem-down notes are performed by tapping both hands on your lap. Stem-up notes are performed by clapping your hands together. Next, I will play the music as an accompaniment while you perform Body Percussion 1 (don't forget the repeat sign). Let's try again with Body Percussion 2. Finally, let's switch roles.

GRANNY'S PIE

Cheerfully

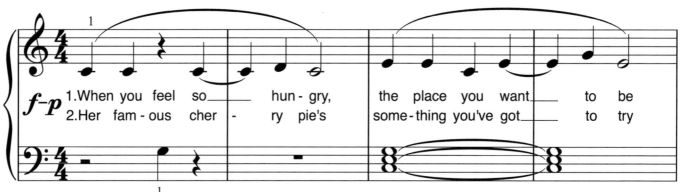

1. When you feel so__ hun-gry, the place you want__ to be
2. Her fam-ous cher - ry pie's some-thing you've got__ to try

is sit-ting hav - ing tea here in Gran-ny's kit - chen.
There is a big__ sup-ply, here in Gran-ny's kit - chen.

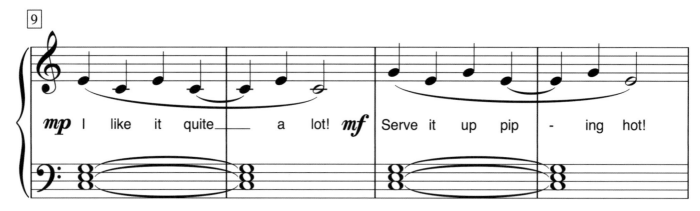

mp I like it quite__ a lot! *mf* Serve it up pip - ing hot!

f Cut me off a slice of Gran-ny's cher - ry pie!

BAD DOG

Traditional, arr. by Andrea Dow

Moodily

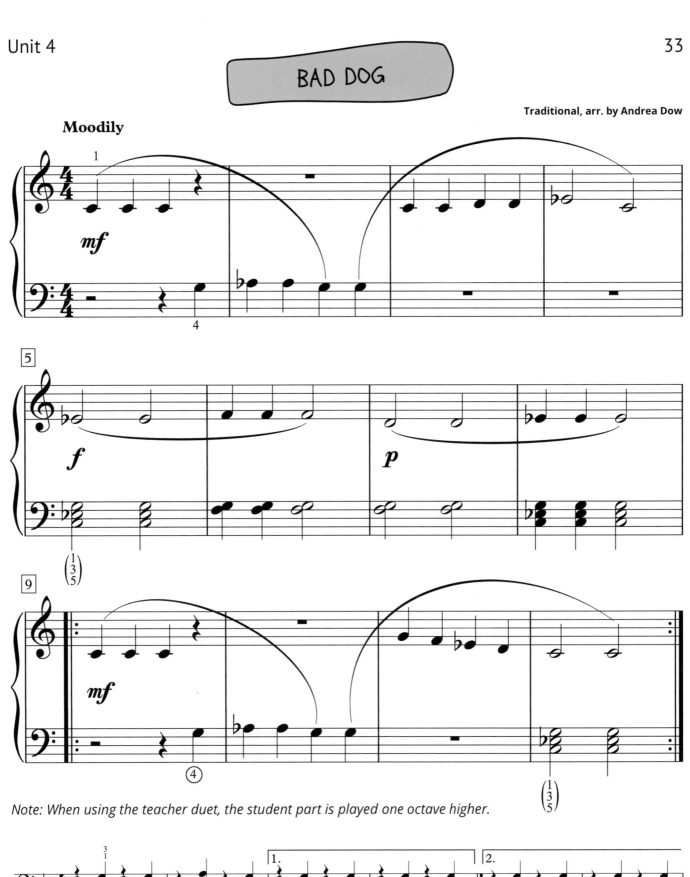

Note: When using the teacher duet, the student part is played one octave higher.

LONELY TONIGHT

Line 2 of this piano piece contains a repeat sign and a first and second ending.
As you repeat the first two lines, ignore the first ending and play the
second ending before moving on to the rest of the piece.

Sadly

Chopin, arr. by Andrea Dow

① **Let's learn about eighth notes.** I will point to the eighth notes below. Two eighth notes equal a quarter note. Before we practice with eighth notes let's learn to count rhythm in a new way.

② Clap and count the first rhythm saying, "One, two, three, four" (the old way). Next, clap and count the first rhythm again saying, "One and two and three and four and" (the new way). Make sure your clapping keeps a steady beat through both measures. Try again.

③ Let's practice clapping and counting eighth notes. In the second rhythm the colored quarter note in the first measure is replaced by **two colored eighth notes** in the second measure. I will show you how to clap and count this rhythm using our new way of counting. Now you try!

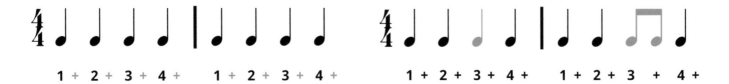

THE MINERS ADD A LITTLE JUICE TO THE PIANO.

Look at the first measure below. I will clap and count the measure using our new way of counting rhythm (one and two and three and four and). Now it's your turn to clap and count the measure.

Next, I will clap and count a new measure. Can you point to the measure I clapped? Let's play again with another measure. **Let's keep playing.**

Beginning at Snow White and ending at the apples, clap and count the four measures of music that rest on the dotted path. Next, with your RH 1 on Middle C play and count the same four measures. I will use a colored crayon to draw a new four-measure path that begins at Snow White and ends at the apples. Try clapping and counting and then playing along the new path. **Let's play again.**

pick-a-path
SIGHT READING

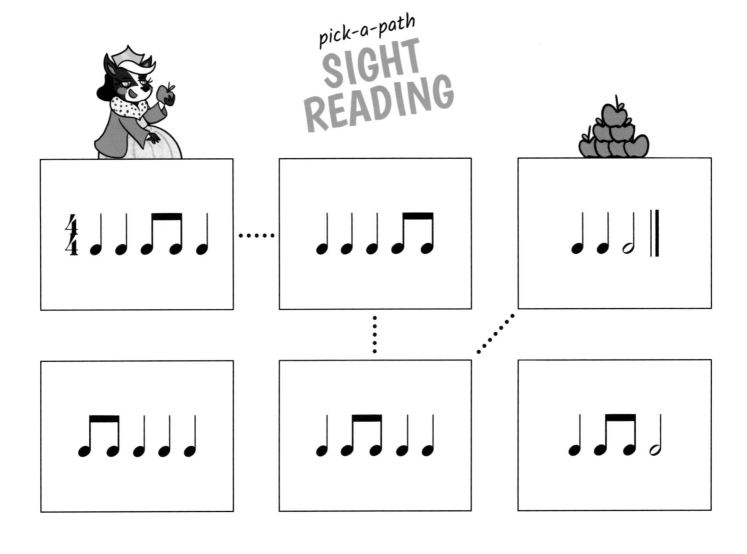

The two measures in Row 1 are **almost identical**. With your RH 1 on Middle C, play and count the first measure of music. Now look at the second measure. The colored quarter note in the first measure has been replaced by two colored eighth notes in the second measure. Play and count the second measure. Practice playing with eighth notes in Rows 2 to 5.

THE MINERS' MUSIC CATCHES THE ATTENTION OF A PASSING PRINCE.

I'M IN NEED OF ROYAL MUSICIANS. WOULD YOU LIKE TO MOVE TO THE PALACE?

Sit on the floor with a red crayon and a blue crayon. Place a finger over any circle and then listen as I clap a measure of rhythm in 4/4 time that contains eighth notes or does not contain eighth notes.

Lift your finger off the circle. If the letter label on the circle **matches** the rhythm I clapped, color the circle red. If the letter label does not match the rhythm I clapped, color the circle blue. Let's keep playing until there are three circles colored red (you win) or three circles colored blue (I win).

ear-training EXERCISE

Game Note: Look at the letters in the circles below. Y means "Yes, it contained eighth notes" and N means "No, it did not contain eighth notes".

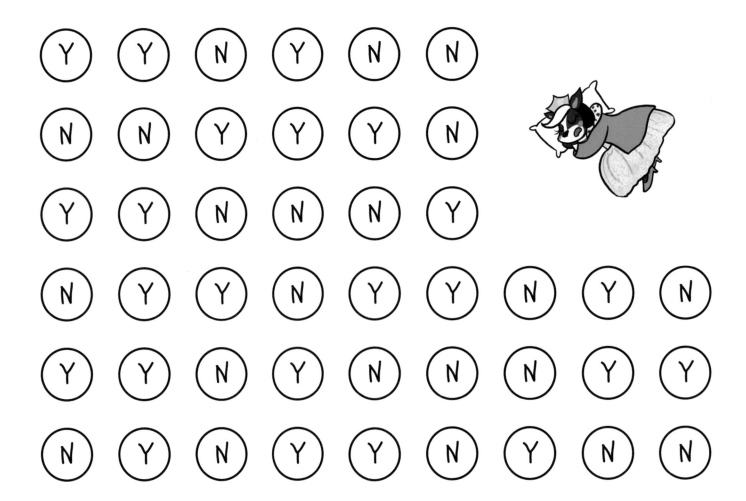

technical EXERCISES

RHYTHM ALERT! When you get to Exercise 3 look at the first measure. In this measure, four eighth notes are tied together with a single beam. I will show you how to clap and count this measure. Now you try. Next, let's clap and count all of Exercise 3.

COOK AND CLEAN

Brightly

Yes, I do con-fess that there is a mess but I hate to cook and clean!

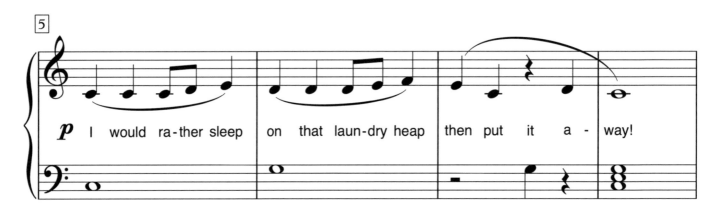

I would ra-ther sleep on that laun-dry heap then put it a - way!

Just leave the dish-es there in the sink. I'll wash them in the mor-ning.

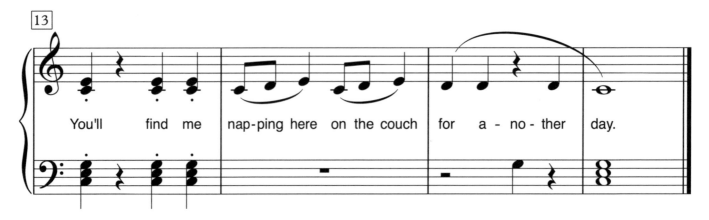

You'll find me nap-ping here on the couch for a - no - ther day.

Brightly

Vivaldi, arr. by Andrea Dow

Note: When using the teacher duet, the student part is played one octave higher.

POISON APPLES

Steadily

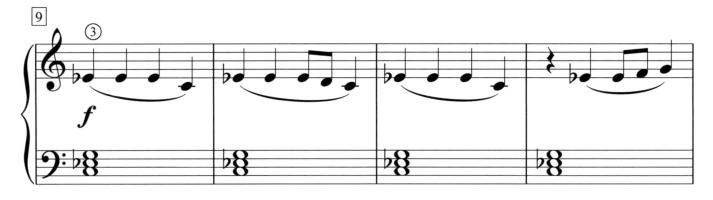

let's get STARTED

1 We've been exploring C five-finger scales. Now it's time to learn a new five-finger scale. Look at the **G five-finger scale** on the treble staff below. You already know Treble G, C and D. Can you tap every Treble G? C? D?

2 To play this scale you only need to learn two new notes. Treble A and B are above Treble G. These two notes are colored in the music below. I will point to Treble A. Next, I will point to Treble B.

3 Listen as I play the line of music. Now it's your turn! With your RH 1 on Treble G, play the music. **Say the note names** as you play.

I will point to a measure of music below. Can you **name the notes** on the treble staff? Let's play again with a different measure.

Next, look at the bass staff of each measure. Can you name the only note that appears? It's **Bass G.**

Place your LH 5 on Bass G and your RH 1 on Treble G. Next, follow the instructions below.

Beginning at the bear and ending at the school, play the four measures of music that rest on the dotted path. Next, I will use a colored crayon to draw a new four-measure path that begins at the bear and ends at the school. Try playing along the new path. **Let's play again.**

technical EXERCISES

Read this before you play Exercise 3! You've played D above Middle C many times with your right hand, but did you know that it can be played with your left hand too? When it is played with your left hand it looks different because the note head rests above the Middle C line. Can you find D above Middle C in Exercise 3?

Let's practice listening for **eighth notes** in 3/4 and 4/4 time. To begin, I will secretly choose five numbers between one and thirty-six, record them on a slip of paper, and hide the paper until the game is over.

Next, listen as I play a measure of music in 3/4 or 4/4 time. Tell me the name of the time signature I played and then roll a die. If I played in 4/4 time, color a number of **squares** below that corresponds to the value on the die. If I played in 3/4 time, color a number of **circles** below that corresponds to the value on the die. Let's play three more rounds.

ear-training EXERCISE

Scoring the Game: After all rounds are complete, I will reveal the secret numbers. Examine the numbers inside each shape below. Score yourself one point for every colored shape that contains a secret number.

Note to Teachers: This game requires you to improvise musical excerpts in 3/4 and 4/4 time that contain eighth notes. Below are two examples of measures that you may consider playing.

Example measures only (remember the repeat):

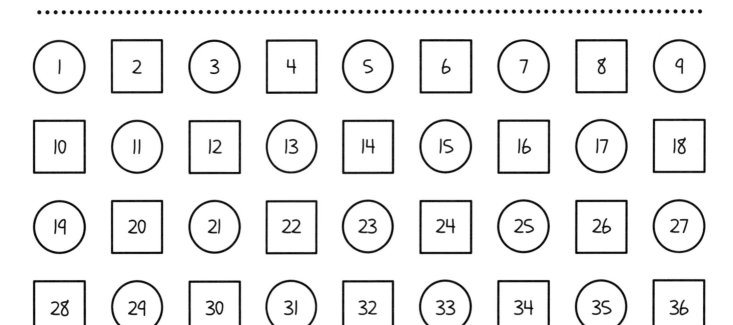

Let's play a Rhythm Duet! To begin, practice Body Percussions 1 and 2 below. Stem-down notes are performed by tapping both hands on your lap. Stem-up notes are performed by clapping your hands together. Next, I will play the music as an accompaniment while you perform Body Percussion 1 (don't forget the repeat sign). Let's try again with Body Percussion 2. Finally, let's switch roles.

ENTER THE BEAR

FOREST FRIENDS

Cheerfully

Bach, arr. by Andrea Dow

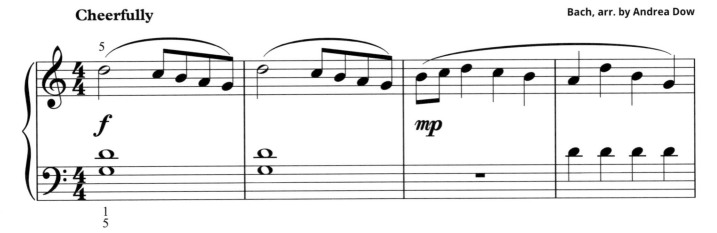

Note: When using the teacher duet, the student part is played one octave higher.

BROKEN BENCH

Brooding

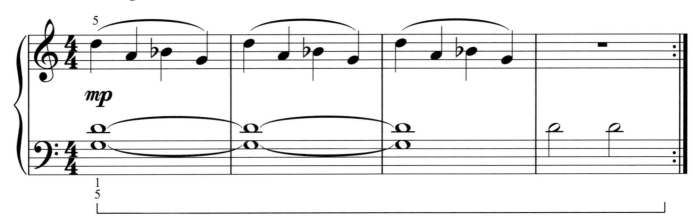

let's get **STARTED**

1 The first G five-finger scale below begins on Treble G. You learned this scale in the last unit. Now let's learn a **new G five-finger scale!**

2 The G five-finger scale in the second excerpt begins on Bass G and ends on D above Middle C. You played with these two notes in the last unit. The remaining notes in this scale are A, B, and C. You already know these notes too. They are the **colored notes** on the bass staff.

3 Below the staves are Roman Numeral names for the notes. Can you play the first scale? The second scale? Say the note names as you play.

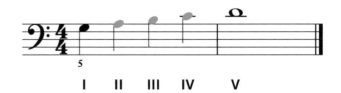

With your LH 5 on Bass G, play the I, III and V notes of the G major five-finger scale at the same time. This is called a **blocked** G major chord.

Next, with your LH 5 on Bass G, play the I, III and V notes of the G major five-finger scale one after another. This is called a **broken** G major chord.

Can you find a blocked G major chord below? Can you find a broken G major chord below?

Beginning at the duckling and ending at the sign, play the four measures of music that rest on the dotted path. Next, I will use a colored crayon to draw a new four-measure path that begins at the duckling and ends at the sign. Try playing along the new path. **Let's play again.**

technical EXERCISES

THEORY TIME! If a flat sign is placed on the III note of a G major five-finger scale, it becomes a G minor five-finger scale. If a flat sign is placed on the III note of a G major chord, it becomes a G minor chord. Practice playing these minor sounds in Exercise 3.

MAMA DUCK IS FEELING CONCERNED.

DARLING, YOU HAVEN'T LEARNED TO SWIM, FISH OR FLY. WHAT ARE YOU GOING TO DO?

Listen as I play a broken G major chord or a broken G minor chord. Locate the box below that corresponds to the chord I played, and roll a die. Inside the selected box, **color a numbered circle** that corresponds to the number rolled. If all circles that correspond to the number rolled have already been colored in previous rounds, draw an **X** over one blue circle.

Next, repeat the procedure above until all of the circles inside one of the two boxes are colored or until there is an **X** over every blue circle.

ear-training
EXERCISE

Winning the Game: The student wins the game if all of the circles in one of the two boxes are colored before an **X** is drawn over every blue circle.

MAJOR   MINOR

MAJOR			MINOR		
1	5	3	2	1	3
3	M	1	5	m	2
2	4	4	1	4	6

Let's play a Rhythm Duet! To begin, practice Body Percussions 1 and 2 below. Stem-down notes are performed by tapping both hands on your lap. Stem-up notes are performed by clapping your hands together. Next, I will play the music as an accompaniment while you perform Body Percussion 1 (don't forget the repeat sign). Let's try again with Body Percussion 2. Finally, let's switch roles.

FEATHER IN THE WIND

Flowing

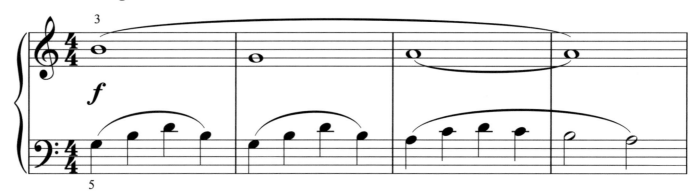

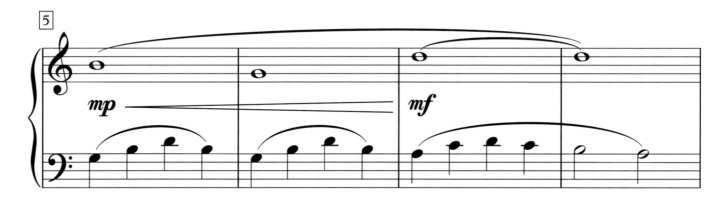

Gently

Beethoven, arr. by Andrea Dow

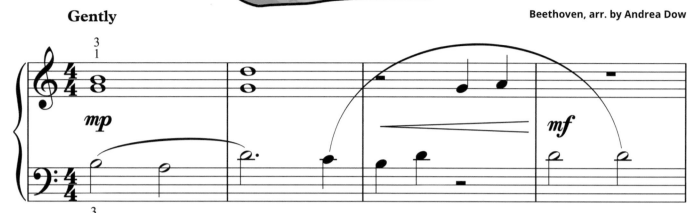

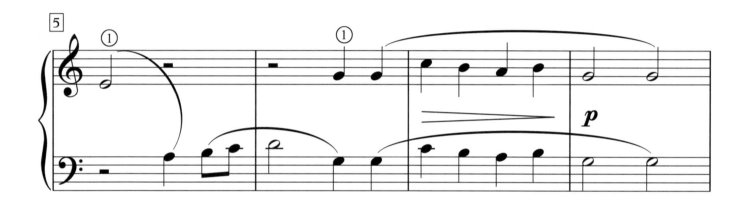

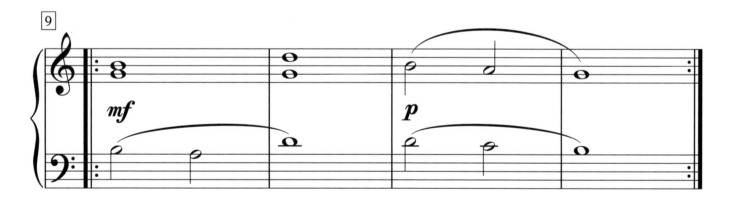

Note: When using the teacher duet, the student part is played one octave higher.

TOP HAT TANGO

With Excitement

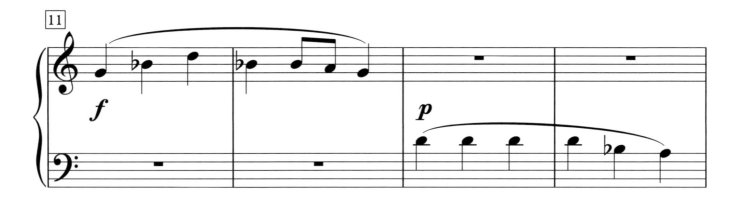

let's get STARTED

1 With your LH 5 on Bass G, play the first musical excerpt below. Play it again. Play it again with your **eyes closed**. Next, move your LH 5 to Low G (Low Bass G). Close your eyes and play the same musical pattern one more time.

2 **Guess what?** You just played the second musical excerpt using three new notes: Low G, Low A, and Low B!

3 Look at the second musical excerpt. Low G is a line note like Treble G, Low A is a space note like Treble A, and Low B is a line note like Treble B.

G   A   B   A   B   A   G

Look at the measures of music below. Point to every measure that has an A on the bass staff. Point to every measure that has a B on the bass staff.

Next, tap every Low G in the measures of music. Tap every Treble G in the measures of music.

Use the finger-number clues in the music below to find your starting position. Next, I will point to a random measure of music for you to play. Let's try again with the remaining measures.

Beginning at the mamba and ending at the worm wizard, play the four measures of music that rest on the dotted path. Next, I will use a colored crayon to draw a new four-measure path that begins at the mamba and ends at the worm wizard. Try playing along the new path. **Let's play again.**

pick-a-path
SIGHT READING

technical EXERCISES

NOTE-READING ALERT! Look at the first measure of music in Exercise 3. It combines the three new notes you learned on pages 59 and 60 (Low G, A and B) with two notes you already know (Bass C and D) to create a G five-finger scale. Practice playing this new scale before performing Exercise 3.

You now know how to play four Gs on the piano (Low G, Bass G, Treble G, High G). The distance between a key and the very next key with the same name represents an **interval of an octave.**

Listen as I play Bass G and then the key that is an octave higher. Listen as I play Bass G and then the key that is an octave lower. Now let's play a game!

Note to Teachers: The game below requires you to play an octave moving higher, an octave moving lower or an interval that is not an octave.

ear-training
EXERCISE

Place a coin over the mongoose. Listen as I play an interval. Move your coin one space to the right if I played an octave moving higher, one space to the left if I played an octave moving lower, and one space forward if I played an interval that is not an octave.

Next, I will keep playing until your coin lands on any **red circle** (you win) or a **mamba** (you lose). If your coin lands on a green circle, it is returned to the mongoose and play continues.

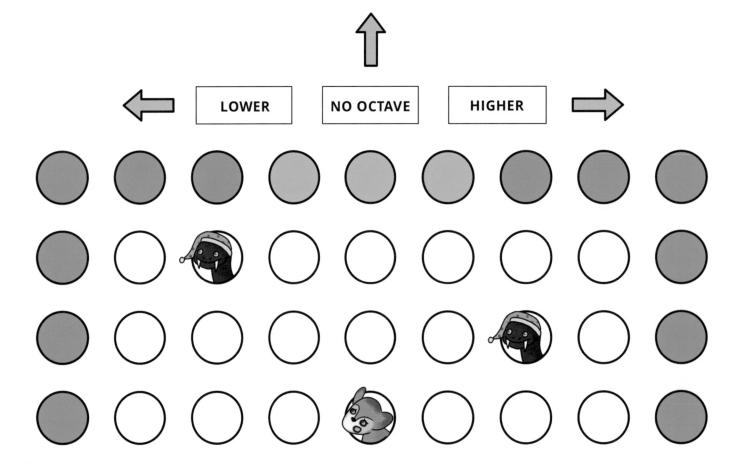

Let's play a Rhythm Duet! To begin, practice Body Percussions 1 and 2 below. Stem-down notes are performed by tapping both hands on your lap. Stem-up notes are performed by clapping your hands together. Next, I will play the music as an accompaniment while you perform Body Percussion 1 (don't forget the repeat sign). Let's try again with Body Percussion 2. Finally, let's switch roles.

MAMBA MOTION

Bluesy

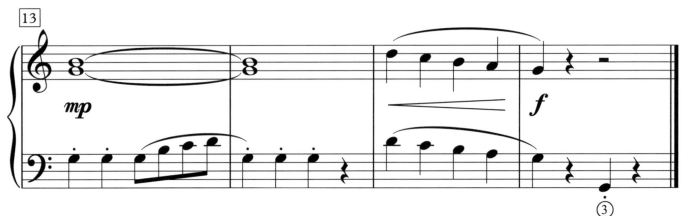

A FRIENDLY FOE

Mozart, arr. by Andrea Dow

Note: When using the teacher duet, the student part is played one octave higher.

THE WORM WIZARD

Mysteriously